Use a Holistic Approach, Not a Single Magic Fix

Dr. Yi Song

ISBN: 979-8-9948506-7-1 (print)

Regeneration Effect Publishing

This is Book Six of

Regeneration Effect :

Sacred Wisdom for Staying Young

BOOK 6

A holistic approach sees the body as an **integrated terrain**. Not a machine with replaceable parts, but a living, breathing **ecosystem**.

Every cell, every system, every sensation is part of a greater whole. The immune system doesn't function in a vacuum. It depends on the **gut**. The brain doesn't think clearly

without the **heart's rhythm** and the **breath's pace**. And your emotional state?

 It leaves fingerprints everywhere. From your **digestion** to your **posture**, from your **hormones** to the **expression on your face**. When we say "holistic," we don't mean vague or mystical.

We mean **honest**.

We mean **complete.**

Because the body doesn't separate its processes the way textbooks do.

You don't grieve in your mind alone. You grieve in your **lungs**, your **belly**, your **bones**. You don't love just with your heart. You love with your immune system, your skin, your voice, your presence.

So when we talk about *true* holistic health, we're talking about something much deeper than just a checklist of supplements or habits.

We're talking about:

- **Preventive care rooted in rhythm— not crisis management.** Not waiting for something to break before you start paying attention. Honoring the *natural flow* of your body, the seasons, the sleep-wake cycle, and the subtle signs that something needs adjusting.

- **Whole foods that support biological intelligence—not isolated nutrients.** Eating with reverence for the *wholeness* of plants, herbs, and traditional dishes. Foods that carry not just calories, but *coded information.* The kind your body recognizes and knows exactly how to use.

- **Movement, breath, rest, and relationships as medicine—not just lifestyle.** Treating your daily walk like therapy. Your sleep like a sacred ceremony. Your community like a nutrient. Your breath like a bridge between the visible and invisible.

- **And an understanding that nature is not separate from us—it's the**

blueprint we were built from. The

patterns in the trees, the tides, the animal

migrations. They're mirrored inside us.

The body isn't just *in* nature. It **is** nature.

A truly holistic approach addresses the body, mind, and spirit as an interconnected system—one that cannot be compartmentalized.

This isn't about chasing forever. It's about reclaiming quality of life, especially in your later years.

When I started my holistic clinic 20 years ago, I set my goal of **educating as many people as possible** about the principle of early prevention and treating the root cause

of conditions preached in The *Yellow

Emperor's Classic of Medicine*.

Sadly, in the past twenty years of practicing,

**I've found that most people have no

interest in making an effort toward early

prevention.**

Most people's minds are deeply rooted in

the modern Western Medicine model

established around 150 years ago.

**Most people today believe that

modern Western medicine has a**

solution for every problem—no matter when it appears.

Got high blood pressure? There's a pill for that.

Cholesterol too high? Another prescription.

In this mindset, there's little incentive to take responsibility early. Many see no real issue with eating processed foods, drinking regularly, smoking, or avoiding exercise. Deep down, they know these habits are harmful, **but comfort has become their**

normal. The thought of giving up what feels good now for the sake of a healthier body years later feels too distant, too abstract.

And change—real change—takes effort.

It takes effort to get up and move when it's easier to sit. It takes effort to walk past the fast food and reach for something fresh and nourishing. Most people know what they *should* do, but they don't have the will—or the urgency—to do it.

Because change only happens when the pain of staying with the status quo finally outweighs the pain of making changes.

This belief—**that medicine will always fix the damage**—has become a dangerous **illusion**. Many don't see the need to modify behaviors that cause slow, silent harm because everyone around them is living the same way. They see people survive with surgeries, medications, and medical interventions and **assume that's just how life works**.

"Why not enjoy life now?" they ask. "Why give up what feels good if doctors can patch things up later?"

But that's the trap.

When we rely on medicine to fix what could have been prevented, we trade vitality for convenience—and by the time we realize it, **it's often too late.**

The Answer Is Never Medication Alone

If there's one myth we need to debunk, it's

this: **that healing comes in a bottle.** Yes,

medications can save lives. Western

pharmaceuticals are powerful, precise tools

—but they're also **incomplete** when used in

isolation.

 Here's the problem: **pharmaceutical drugs**

are often extracted from plants, refined

into isolated compounds, and then amplified

to target a specific biochemical mechanism.

But in doing so, they remove the buffering

compounds that exist in the whole plant—

compounds that naturally reduce side

effects, enhance bioavailability, and work

synergistically to support the body.

In contrast, **Eastern and functional medicine** approach healing holistically. Herbs, roots, mushrooms, and minerals are used in their natural forms—combined into formulas that balance and support the body as a whole, not just silence a symptom.

Take **qing hao**, the ancient Chinese herb that became the foundation for modern anti-malarial drugs. Once again, one compound was isolated—**artemisinin**—while the rest of the plant was cast aside.

But that "rest" held wisdom too. Balancing compounds. Cooling energetics. Micronutrients we haven't even fully cataloged.

And when people started using artemisinin in isolation, yes, it killed malaria—but over time, it also created resistance.

Nature, when unbalanced, fights back.

Think of it this way:

- **Western model:** Suppress the symptom.

- **Eastern model:** Support the system.

When biohacking borrows from the wisdom of ancient systems—when it uses herbs, adaptogens, natural remedies, and targeted nutrients in their full-spectrum forms—it moves from being just performance optimization to **deep biological support**.

The Biggest Mistake: A Fragmented Approach

Health isn't about isolated hacks or scattered advice. Many people don't know how to truly integrate wellness practices in a way that benefits their unique body.

Understanding your health requires seeing

the full picture, not just individual pieces.

- **What's Not Holistic**

Let's be clear about what doesn't qualify

as truly holistic:

- **Chasing biohacks one at a time**

Jumping from cold plunges to peptides

to red light therapy without

understanding your body's deeper needs

or imbalances creates more *noise* than

clarity. Hacks are tools. Not foundations.

- **Focusing on a single "miracle" supplement or drug** Whether it's Rapamycin, Metformin, or the latest trending adaptogen, no single compound can restore health if the *ecosystem* it's entering is inflamed, exhausted, or disconnected.

- **Targeting one area while neglecting the rest**

- You can't meditate your way out of blood sugar dysregulation. You can't exercise your way out of trauma. The body demands *synergy*, not silos.

A Truly

Holistic

Approach

Is About Systems, Not Symptoms.

In June, one of my mentors fell while protecting her granddaughter from a dog and injured her right shoulder.

Following the conventional path, she went to an orthopedic surgeon, got an MRI, and was told she had a rotator cuff tear.

The solution seemed straightforward: surgery.

Five holes drilled into her shoulder bone, reattachment, and eight weeks in a sling. For someone running her own business and constantly on the move, this would have been a major interruption. But she accepted the diagnosis and scheduled the surgery.

Before the operation, she went on an Alaskan cruise. While there, she met an acupuncturist offering treatments. Out of curiosity, she tried one session. Afterward, he told her something simple yet powerful:

"Your body is designed to heal itself."

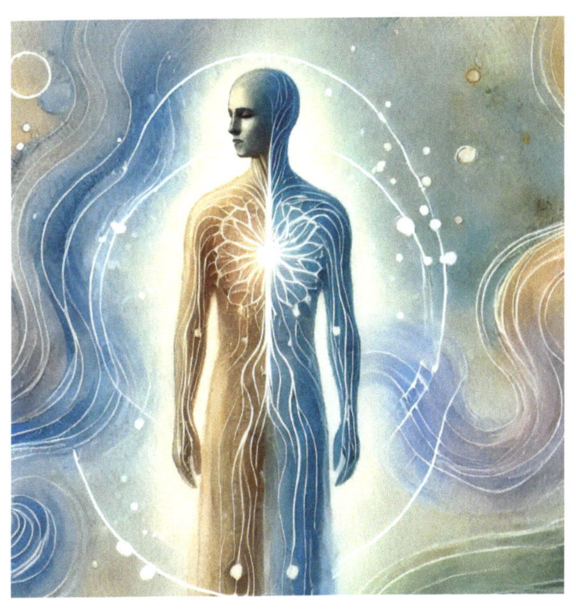

In Chinese medicine, this is often explained

through the movement of energy, or *qi*,

which flows, harmonizes, and nourishes the

body.

She did nine more sessions over the next ten days, and by the end of the cruise she could move her arm significantly better. But when she returned home, she didn't continue treatment. The progress faded, and the pain came back.

That's when she reached out to me.

Her husband asked whether stem cells could help with a rotator cuff tear. Instead, I offered something different. I invited them to a Zoom call and showed him where to

press certain pressure points to reduce her
pain.

Because here's the truth we often forget:

Everything in your body is connected.

Your shoulder isn't just your shoulder.

It's part of a system—your garden.

Irrigation channels run throughout that
garden, and when one is blocked, pain can
appear far from the source.

I marked a point on her leg that
corresponded to the shoulder. When her

husband pressed it, she suddenly lifted her arm without pain. This wasn't magic.

This was her body reminding her that it isn't a machine with isolated parts you can simply lubricate or replace.

It's an interconnected ecosystem, and clearing one blocked channel can transform another area entirely.

I had him do additional points—on her ear, which reflects the entire body's map—pressing for two to five minutes. I sent them an herbal relief spray to support circulation, and recommended a simple hot water bottle at night to increase warmth and flow while she slept.

By mid-October, she told me her shoulder was *mostly recovered.* This was remarkable considering that, just a month prior, **the surgeon insisted she needed immediate surgery to regain movement.**

Her experience is a reminder that sometimes healing comes from approaches we aren't familiar with. Not because Western medicine is wrong, but because it sees only **part of the picture**.

When you understand your whole self—your constitution, your patterns, your energy, your emotional landscape—**you expand your possibilities.**

Open-mindedness doesn't mean trying everything. It means being willing to explore what aligns with your body's design.

Because healing isn't about choosing one

system over another—**it's about knowing**

yourself well enough to recognize which

path your body is asking for.

The whole purpose of any treatment—

whether stem cells, red light, herbs,

peptides, acupuncture, or even breathwork—

is not to replace your body's intelligence,

but to *support it*. Stem cells can act as a

spark, a jumpstart, a catalyst. Technologies

can enhance cellular communication. Herbs

can ground and nourish. But none of them

do the healing for you.

Your body is designed to heal itself.

Your job is to create the environment where that healing becomes possible.

And that environment looks different for everyone.

Your constitution, your history, your emotions, your habits, the way you digest food, the way you handle stress—they all shape the internal landscape where regeneration either thrives or struggles.

That's why "one method" will never be enough.

True longevity comes from weaving together the right methods for *your* unique system.

This is where your Personal Codes come in:

A set of practices, tools, and rhythms that align with your biology and help your healing unfold naturally.

To get in-depth discussion about your own
Holistic Approach, scan the QR code to
preorder "Regeneration Effect: Sacred
Wisdom for Staying Young" and learn how
you can implement all the principles in
your life.

ABOUT THE AUTHOR

Dr. Yi Song was born and raised in Beijing, China, into a family with seventeen generations of experience in both Chinese and Western medicine. Twenty-eight years ago, she came to the United States to study pathology at Brown University. After observing the shortcomings of symptom-focused treatments, Dr. Song returned to her roots to focus on true regenerative healing — addressing disease at its source. She has had a holistic clinic in Boston since 2004. In

2018, she founded the Zenerchi Retreat in Medellin, Colombia. Her introduction to stem cell therapy in 2020 was marked by her mother's successful treatment and subsequent independence at age 81. Dr. Song believes that stem cell therapy aligns with holistic principles and is the author of "Regeneration Effect: Sacred Wisdom for Staying Young" and the series of seven books in "The Six Principles to Natural Longevity". Her vision is to combine stem cell therapy, Traditional Chinese Medicine, and anti-aging treatments to help people live a long, high-quality life. She offers advanced stem cell treatments at Zenerchi Retreat in Colombia not available in the US. You can also get consultation about your conditions and concerns in person in Boston or at our network of doctors in the US and online.